Avie's Hope

Lisa M. Hall

Archway Publishing books may be ordered through booksellers or by contacting:

Archway Publishing
1663 Liberty Drive
Bloomington, IN 47403
www.archwaypublishing.com
844-669-3957

Because of the dynamic nature of the Internet, any web addresses or links contained in this book may have changed since publication and may no longer be valid. The views expressed in this work are solely those of the author and do not necessarily reflect the views of the publisher, and the publisher hereby disclaims any responsibility for them.

ISBN: 978-1-6657-7179-5 (sc)
ISBN: 978-1-6657-7178-8 (hc)
ISBN: 978-1-6657-7177-1 (e)

Library of Congress Control Number: 2025900668

Print information available on the last page.

Archway Publishing rev. date: 02/11/2025

Foreword

Working with children each day whose lives have been impacted by substance abuse disorders, I have firsthand witnessed the power of horses to transform their lives. Substance abuse disorder has devastating impacts on the person struggling with the disorder and their loved ones, especially children.

Horses are incredibly effective in helping children and adults overcome and make lasting changes to limiting thoughts, perceptions, beliefs and patterns of behavior that often develop as a result of substance abuse disorder. Lisa Hall has captured the essence of how horses bring hope to the lives of the broken hearted in Avie's Hope.

Hope for Hearts Farm is a non-profit Equine Assisted-learning program, and the home for Jake, Rosie, Rizzo and Will in this story. These horses have given hope and changed thousands of lives over the years, just like the horses in Avie's story changed her life, giving her confidence and hope for her future.

Lisa Bowman
President & Lead Facilitator
Hope for Hearts Farm, Inc.

While Avie's Hope is a work of fiction, it portrays a reality that educators, caregivers, and community members encounter every day. Many children face the invisible burden of growing up in homes impacted by addiction, grappling with emotions they may not have the words to express. This book sheds light on their experiences, reminding us of the vital role we play in offering understanding, support, and hope. Let Avie's story serve as a call to action, inspiring us to build a future where every child feels seen, valued, and loved.

Dr. Laura Hammack
Superintendent, Beech Grove City Schools

About the Author

Award winning first time filmmaker, Lisa Hall created the concept for "The Addict's Wake" and Avie's Hope, to give voice to this nation's struggle of declining mental health and Substance Abuse Disorder .With a background in non-profit leadership, and experience working with women in incarceration she is deeply committed to the message of the film series and Avie's Hope. For her work with the documentary film she has garnered the Distinguished Hoosier Award, National recognition with Public Broadcasting Systems, and innumerable awards for "The Addict's Wake".

Acknowledgments

My thanks and gratitude go the following individuals who have supported my dream for this story.

-Marianne Metzelaar, my angel and editor!

-Ron Carter who helped me get unstuck one July day at a conference.

-To a resilient young woman who bravely shared her journey.

And to my Payton Marie, Paisley Marilyn, Avery Joy and Brooks Ezra- you are the brightest lights in my world and I love being your CoCo. I want a nothing more for you than healthy and full lives free of substances that so easily entangle. I love you to the moon, the stars and to the sun and back.... times a million.

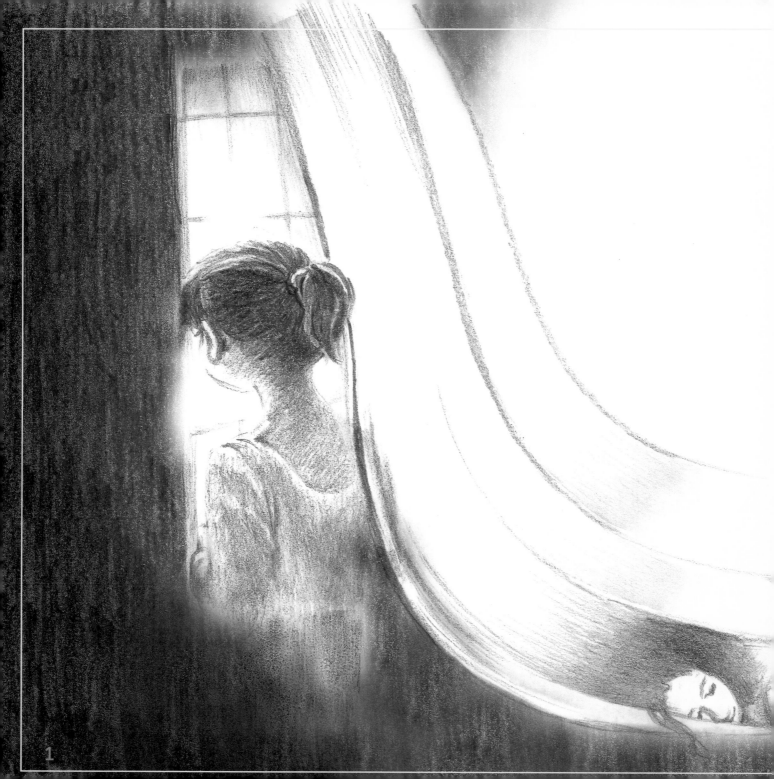

Dad:
Avie, why so unhappy on this beautiful day?
Don't you wish to go out and play?

Avie:
I'm feeling sad, sad, sad and I must say
there's no one to play with on this day.

Baby brother is crying
and I tried the rocking chair.
He might be hungry. . .he needs love and care.

I tried to wake Mommy
because Brooks needs her touch.
I'm just his sissy and cannot offer much.

Mommy will sleep all day.
If I awake her, she will tell me to go away.

2

Dad:
What would you do with your mom if you could?

Avie:
I'd love to ride bikes through our neighborhood.
I would peddle as fast as I can,
feeling the wind in my face just like a fan.

Dad:
I am so sorry Avie that I had to go...
I want you to know that I love you so.

Avie:
I miss your smile and all of your ways. . .
I loved your pancakes to start my days.

Dad:

I'm so sorry that your life is hard.
I know my leaving has left some scars.

Your hurt runs deep but please let hope in
so that your dreams for your life
can surely begin.

You are sweet, caring and kind
and you have a very creative mind.

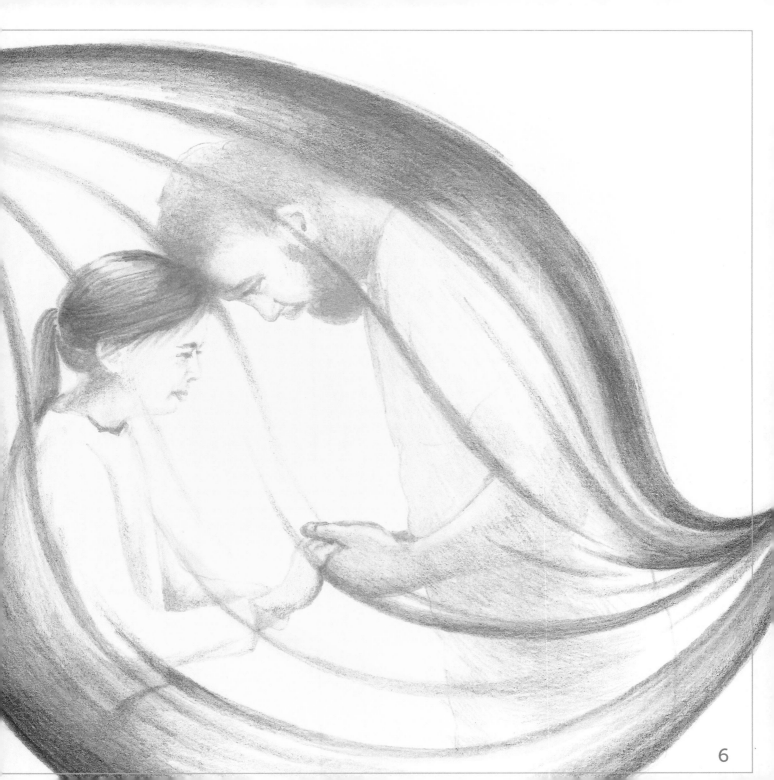

6

Avie:
There are times when I don't know
who will be at my house.
Some days I just want to scream and shout!

Nana stays with me the most
when Mommy is not there.
She loves to add bows and clips to my hair!

Avie:

Nana and granddad do many things for me.
They try so hard but really don't see.

The things that my heart really aches for
are not the things that are bought in a store.

Avie:
There's a new man living in my house
and it makes me mad.
He is so different than you, dad.

Dad:
Not so fast...maybe he is cool?
What if he can help you with your school?

Avie:
Mommy says we may have to move again,
not knowing where their new jobs take them.

Dad:
Let's you and I think about this anew
and remember all of those who truly love you ~
There's Nana, Auntie, Granddad, Uncle Fred
and that sweet friend of yours whose hair is red!

Avie:
That's Samantha! Sam for short,
and she is my best friend I am happy to report!

Avie:

We can't forget Prince, my favorite horse in my head.
I imagine him the most when I am feeling such dread.

Prince is the greatest horse of them all. . .
He is there for me and neighs loudly when I call.

Dad:
I want to remind you that you are not to blame.
There is no need to carry any shame.

Your mom and I let the drugs in. . .
We could not have known what that choice
would begin.

Avie:

I know, and I want Mommy to get well.
I'm glad I have Nana and my teacher to tell.

Sometimes when I still feel so sad,
I can talk with them without feeling bad.

15

Avie:

My teacher tells me I'm strong and brave as well,
my make-believe horses and I have stories to tell!

I love my dreams where we dance, laugh and play.
They make me feel safe and my sadness goes away.

I play with Prince, and his friends
Jake, Rosie, Rizzo and Will...
I never ever want to take those pills!

Dad:
Your life is important and you are free
to become any person you want to be.

Your Mom's and my choices along the way
do not have to be yours tomorrow or any day!

Avie:
It's not easy, but I will do my best
so that I can find my own peace and rest.

I do believe that my life is mine.
With the memories of you, Nana,
Sam and my horses,
I will be just fine!